EXERCISE
Your
FAITH

30 Devotions to Help Strengthen Your Walk Physically and Spiritually

ROBIN URBINA

WestBow
PRESS
A DIVISION OF THOMAS NELSON
& ZONDERVAN

Copyright © 2023 Robin Urbina.

All rights reserved. No part of this book may be used or reproduced by any means, graphic, electronic, or mechanical, including photocopying, recording, taping or by any information storage retrieval system without the written permission of the author except in the case of brief quotations embodied in critical articles and reviews.

This book is a work of non-fiction. Unless otherwise noted, the author and the publisher make no explicit guarantees as to the accuracy of the information contained in this book and in some cases, names of people and places have been altered to protect their privacy.

WestBow Press books may be ordered through booksellers or by contacting:

WestBow Press
A Division of Thomas Nelson & Zondervan
1663 Liberty Drive
Bloomington, IN 47403
www.westbowpress.com
844-714-3454

Because of the dynamic nature of the Internet, any web addresses or links contained in this book may have changed since publication and may no longer be valid. The views expressed in this work are solely those of the author and do not necessarily reflect the views of the publisher, and the publisher hereby disclaims any responsibility for them.

Any people depicted in stock imagery provided by Getty Images are models, and such images are being used for illustrative purposes only. Certain stock imagery © Getty Images.

ISBN: 978-1-6642-9550-6 (sc)
ISBN: 978-1-6642-9549-0 (hc)
ISBN: 978-1-6642-9551-3 (e)

Library of Congress Control Number: 2023905011

Print information available on the last page.

WestBow Press rev. date: 03/27/2023

Scripture quotations marked (ESV) are from the ESV® Bible (The Holy Bible, English Standard Version®), copyright © 2001 by Crossway, a publishing ministry of Good News Publishers. Used by permission. All rights reserved. The ESV text may not be quoted in any publication made available to the public by a Creative Commons license. The ESV may not be translated in whole or in part into any other language.

Scripture quotations marked (NIV) are taken from the Holy Bible, New International Version®, NIV®. Copyright © 1973, 1978, 1984, 2011 by Biblica, Inc.® Used by permission of Zondervan. All rights reserved worldwide. www.zondervan.com The "NIV" and "New International Version" are trademarks registered in the United States Patent and Trademark Office by Biblica, Inc.®

Scripture quotations marked (NASB) taken from the (NASB®) New American Standard Bible®, Copyright © 1960, 1971, 1977 by The Lockman Foundation. Used by permission. All rights reserved. lockman.org

Scripture quotations marked HCSB are taken from the Holman Christian Standard Bible®, Used by Permission HCSB ©1999,2000,2002,2003,2009 Holman Bible Publishers. Holman Christian Standard Bible®, Holman CSB®, and HCSB® are federally registered trademarks of Holman Bible Publishers.

Scripture quotations marked (NLT) are taken from the Holy Bible, New Living Translation, copyright ©1996, 2004, 2015 by Tyndale House Foundation. Used by permission of Tyndale House Publishers, Carol Stream, Illinois 60188. All rights reserved.

Scripture marked (KJV) taken from the King James Version of the Bible.

Scripture marked (NKJV) taken from the New King James Version®. Copyright © 1982 by Thomas Nelson. Used by permission. All rights reserved.

To Rene

Thank you for your unending support throughout this whole process. I know I take on a lot of hobbies and interests. You graciously continue to encourage and support me in each and every one of them with love and patience. I love you.

Contents

Introduction xi

Chapter 1	It's a Stretch...	1
Chapter 2	Bread of Life	4
Chapter 3	Mix It Up..	7
Chapter 4	A Dwelling Place	10
Chapter 5	Small Victories	13
Chapter 6	It Takes Time	16
Chapter 7	Why Fellowship?	18
Chapter 8	Endurance...	21
Chapter 9	A Learning Experience	23
Chapter 10	Love Your Bumps	26
Chapter 11	Take Time to Heal	29
Chapter 12	Don't be a Quitter	31
Chapter 13	Get Energized	33
Chapter 14	A Whole Body Workout	35
Chapter 15	Give It a Rest...	38
Chapter 16	Stay Hydrated	41
Chapter 17	Walking Tall...	43
Chapter 18	Just Have Fun..	45
Chapter 19	Persistence Pays Off	48
Chapter 20	Personal Growth	51
Chapter 21	Be Creative..	54
Chapter 22	Just Do It	57
Chapter 23	But It Hurts	60
Chapter 24	Sleep in Peace......................................	63
Chapter 25	Reach for It	66
Chapter 26	Invest in Yourself..................................	69

Chapter 27 Wait for It	72
Chapter 28 A Balancing Act	74
Chapter 29 It Takes Discipline	77
Chapter 30 It's a Narrow Road	80
In Closing	83
Final Thoughts and Encouragement	85
Key Verses	87
Memory Verses	91

Introduction

I was inspired to write this book as I was resting in between laps at my local pool. I love swimming and exercise. I love writing and journaling. Most of all, I love the Lord. My passion in life is to encourage people and inspire them to do things they never think they can do or maybe don't have the courage to do.

This is by no means a professional guide about exercise or a scholarly text about Bible translation and verses. You'll see my personal experiences and feelings while comparing their likenesses to our faith and how they've gotten me through some trying times. Consider this a very elementary and entry level look at where to start and how to grow in your faith.

Please do your own research on exercise and what's best for you. Consult a doctor first if you're not sure how to begin any exercise or nutrition program. I am not a licensed expert on anything. I am not an eloquent speaker nor do I have a great vocabulary, so please grin when you read my simple style of writing. I want to share my thoughts with you and hope I can encourage you today to be a better you, to motivate you to make better food choices, or to help you get through something you've been struggling with. Whether it be food, exercise, or walking with Jesus, I pray these pages make you smile or just give you the desire to keep going. I pray you are inspired to open your Bible, or go for a walk, or even just cry out to God and hear Him speak to you.

Thank you for letting me share.

1
It's a Stretch

Then He said to the man, "Stretch out your hand!" He stretched it out, and it was restored to normal, like the other.
—*Matthew 12:13 (ESV)*

Looking back on my school years, I remember we always had to stretch before the activity in gym class. I used to think, *This is such a waste of time. Let's just get to it!* Of course, I didn't realize it was actually part of the activity. Stretching should be the beginning of whatever we're doing because it brings another level of benefits to our well-being. It prepares our bodies for the stress of exercise. It gives us better range of motion and makes us more flexible. More importantly, it helps reduce the risk of injuries. If you've ever swung a golf club without stretching, I'm sure you've felt a little pain the next day, especially if you haven't played in a long time.

Just as we stretch physically, we must stretch spiritually. This means getting out of our comfort zones. I remember watching the process of being stretched as I prepared for a mission trip to Africa. I never thought God would use me for something so important. I remember when the opportunity came up, and when I realized it was really going to happen. I loved the experience and the journey of being stretched. I watched all the pieces come together, starting with prayer, taking the time off work to be able to go, and raising the funds that were needed. When the time came for us to travel and spend time there, I was stretched even more. I was stretched even further when it came to sharing my testimony or a devotion or just sharing Jesus with the local people. I praise God for that experience and how it increased my faith.

In our key verse in Matthew 12, Jesus didn't just heal the leper; the man had to do something in order to be healed. He heard Jesus, then obeyed with faith. He had to stretch out his withered hand so he could be healed.

God may be asking you to stretch by doing something outside your comfort zone. He may want you to share the gospel with someone you've been afraid to approach. There might be something He wants you to *stop* doing, or He may want you to end something. He may want you to give something. He wants to nudge us out of our comfort zones to prepare us for upcoming challenges. Stretch your faith by turning your fears, doubts, and worries over to Him. Stop thinking something is impossible. There is nothing impossible for God. Trust Him. Don't keep Him in a little box. Stop expecting miracles to happen when you are limiting Him.

Prayer: Sweet heavenly Father, thank You for stretching me. Show me where I need to be stretched. Use me however You see fit. Even though I'm scared, I want You to use me for your glory. Prepare me for what's coming ahead. In Jesus's name, Amen.

Memorize: *Isaiah 40:31 (NIV):* *"But those who hope in the Lord will renew their strength. They will soar on wings like eagles; they will run and not grow weary, they will walk and not be faint."*

Read: 1 Peter 5: 1–11

2
Bread of Life

But he answered, "It is written, 'Man shall not live by bread alone, but by every word that comes from the mouth of God.'"
—*Matthew 4:4 (NIV)*

Wrong food choices and compulsive overeating have always been struggles for me. I never wanted the fruits and vegetables or good proteins that all the experts recommended. The other stuff was comforting and fun, like a best friend I could turn to when I was feeling happy, sad, or any other emotion that I could claim. But when I'm working out, I seem to have a better grip on it. I make better choices because I don't want to "waste my workout." We've all heard the phrases "If I fail to plan, I plan to fail" or "You can't out-exercise your diet." This is so true when considering my food plan. I have to actually think about, and sometimes write down, the food I'm going to eat throughout the day. With a few exceptions like fasting, I think it's safe to say we all eat every day. We need food to satisfy our physical hunger and to give our bodies the energy they need. It's consciously making good choices that is always the challenging part. Here are a few tips to remember.

- When your body is hungry, it wants nutrients, not empty calories. Try not to buy foods or snacks you will regret later.
- If you keep good food in the fridge, you will eat good food. Yes, this means vegetables and fruits. If you're not hungry enough to eat an apple, you're not hungry; you're just bored.
- Keep a food log. This will show you where you need improvement.

Our bodies can experience physical hunger, but our souls experience spiritual hunger. In John 6:35 (ESV), Jesus said, "I am the bread of life; whoever comes to me shall not hunger, and whoever believes in me shall never thirst." Having the right relationship with Jesus allows Him to satisfy our spiritual hunger. We need to be fed spiritually every day. We are faced with temptation every day, and for some, multiple times a day. If we feed ourselves scripture, we will be better equipped to ward off temptation, whether it be in the form of food or other struggles.

Consider our memory verse for today. First Corinthians 10:13 (NIV) says, "No temptation has overtaken you except what is common to mankind. And God is faithful; he will not let you be tempted beyond what you can bear. But when you are tempted, he will also provide a way out so that you can endure it." He is not saying He will not give you circumstances you can't handle. He's saying He will give you the ability and everything you need to handle anything.

Robin Urbina

Prayer: Dear Lord, You know my struggles both physically and emotionally. You know I'm out of control. Thank You, Lord, for being the Bread of Life. Fill me with Your Word. Let it be satisfying to me so I don't run to food today. Satisfy me with what I need so that I can overcome today's temptations. In Jesus's name, Amen.

Memorize: *1 Corinthians 10:13 (NIV): "No temptation has overtaken you except what is common to mankind. And God is faithful; he will not let you be tempted beyond what you can bear. But when you are tempted, he will also provide a way out so that you can endure it."*

Read: John 6:22–40

3
Mix It Up

*Worship the Lord with gladness; come
before him with joyful songs.*
—Psalm 100:2 (NIV)

Swimming is probably my favorite type of exercise. I love how it takes my mind off everything else that might be consuming me. It makes me focus on nothing else but being in the water, being outside, breathing, maintaining the proper form, and counting my strokes. However, I can get bored very easily. That's why I try to find different things to do where I can get in a good workout. Hiking is another favorite. Being in the woods, walking, climbing, stepping over rocks, hearing the stream flowing next to me, seeing wildlife, and feeling the change in temperature has such a peaceful, calming effect. It allows me to slow down and not just look for God but to be in awe of Him and what He created. On the flip side of that, I like to partake in some more adventurous types of activities, like riding a dirt bike. I relish the challenge of manhandling a 240-pound dirt bike over rocks, sand, and trails. Engaging in different activities keeps it fun. Things don't get boring. I always learn something new or see something different.

One of my go-to things to do is dance. Every time my sister and I get together, we have to dance. It's a riot. It's a great workout, and we have a blast. She's over there trying to moonwalk while I'm doing all I can to catch my breath from dancing and laughing at the same time. At the end of our "night out" (in my living room), we're spent. We have a great time all while torching a few calories.

Worshipping and praising God can come in many different forms. It can be through music, serving others, praying, reading, giving, or memorizing verses. God knows our hearts. He knows when we're praising Him. He knows when we're crying out to Him or listening to Him—and He loves it! Listening to gospel music or any type of praise music makes my heart leap. I love reading God's Word. But I know I have to mix it up at times because I don't want to get stale or too comfortable. If I'm in a season of struggle, I know it's time to break it up and try something else. Starting a new book study or maybe a character study always keeps it fresh for me.

Find something interesting and fun that will bring you closer to God. Give your time to someone, or do something for someone in need. You'll find yourself being drawn closer and closer to God so you can live more for Him.

Prayer: Heavenly Father, You know it's easy for me to get bored and stagnant. Open my heart to new ways to worship You. I need some variety. Lead me to a place where I can grow in my walk with You. Lead me to a place

Exercise Your Faith

where I can be a light to others. Start a fire in me so I don't get stale. Thank You for molding me into the person You want me to be. In Jesus's name, Amen.

Memorize: *Matthew 4:10 (NIV): "Jesus said to him, 'Away from me, Satan! For it is written: "Worship the Lord your God, and serve him only."'"*

Read: Hebrews 12:14-28

4
A Dwelling Place

Do you not know that your body is a temple of the Holy Spirit within you, whom you have from God? You are not your own, for you were bought with a price. So glorify God in your body.
—1 Corinthians 19–20 (ESV)

It's taken me a long time to understand the concept of my body being a dwelling place for my Jesus. That thought is all I need to remember when I'm struggling with food. The older I get, the more I understand and appreciate the fact that I need to respect the body God has blessed me with. Yes, I said "blessed me with." I used to make jokes about my body but now I try to honor and respect my Creator by honoring and taking care of it. Eating is a form of self-respect. So is exercise. So is what we feed our thoughts and minds.

A daily practice for me is reading positive affirmations that I've written for myself. I read one a day and they are specific to me. I think we're all guilty of self-destructive thoughts or practices. I am very careful in allowing

Exercise Your Faith

anything that might be negative or anything that might not be pleasing to the Father to dwell in my head. God doesn't make mistakes. I am not a mistake and the way He made me is not a mistake. He created each and every one of us to be unique in our own special ways. He knows our thoughts before we even think them. He knows the number of hairs on our heads (Luke 12:7 NIV). I find it fascinating that the Creator of the Universe knows me intimately and created me to be special, unique, and perfect in His eyes. That alone makes me want to repay him, in a sense, as to thank him. It encourages me to want to serve Him.

In the first part of today's verse, Paul reminds us that when we become Christians, our bodies become temples for the Holy Spirit. The Holy Spirit is what leads us in our choices. In the second part, he reminds us that we were bought for a price—the price Jesus paid when He died on the cross for our sins. It's like renting a house. If I live in a place that belongs to somebody else, I'm going to do all I can to live by and respect their rules, not mine. In its actual context, Paul is talking about fleeing from sexual immorality. However, the idea is that whatever we see or hear or speak should be aligned with God's view. Allowing negativity, hurtful words, and unforgiveness only prolongs the peace that Jesus wants for us.

Paul wrote to the Colossians (3:16 ESV) and instructed them to "Let the Word of Christ dwell in you richly in all wisdom; teaching and admonishing one another in psalms and hymns and spiritual songs, singing with grace in your hearts to the Lord." These words describe people so full of the Word of God that their entire being is affected. When we fill ourselves with the Word, we are enlightened. It's God speaking to us directly. This is how we hear what God wants for us. He nourishes and strengthens us through His Word. Open it today and let Him speak to you.

Prayer: Dear Heavenly Father, thank you for creating me and making me unique and so very special. Thank you for living within me. Father, help me recognize what is negative or not good for my soul and help me rid them from my life. Show me where I have unforgiveness, even in myself, or anything preventing me from fully experiencing your peace. In Jesus' name, Amen.

Memorize: John 14:23 (NIV): "Jesus answered and said to him, 'If anyone loves Me, he will keep My word; and My Father will love him, and We will come to him and make Our abode with him.'"

Read: Ephesians 3:14-21

5
Small Victories

"I have said these things to you, that in me you may have peace. In the world you will have tribulation. But take heart; I have overcome the world."
—John 16:33 (ESV)

As a sugar addict, eating behaviors like compulsive overeating, binging, and purging can be very defeating. It's very lonely. It seems like nobody really understands how bad it can be. I think of fear in the same way. It can be paralyzing.

A friend and I once went to an indoor rock climbing gym. She had never been and was excited to experience something new. At some point, she mentioned she was afraid of heights. I didn't think much of it because she was really excited to try it, but I could see she was still a little nervous. We checked in and got ready for a quick lesson. They showed us how to put the gear on and explained how it worked. They taught us about the different colored holds, which represented different routes you could take while climbing up the wall. After the training session, we were ready to climb. I could see she was a little more anxious but still into it. We took turns climbing and belaying, going higher and higher each time. As she ascended the wall, her demeanor changed from nervous and anxious to happy and proud. She had overcome her fear and felt like she had conquered the world.

When we have challenges that we want to overcome, we have to learn to set small goals. Pray for courage to overcome them. Then set bigger goals. Helen Keller once said, "All the world is full of suffering. It is also full of overcoming."

Nowhere in the Bible does it say we won't suffer heartache or adversities. They are parts of life. They exist to test our faith and to shape us. Our verse today is about the peace believers can get when they rely on Jesus. He says straight up in John 16:33 that we *will* have tribulation. However, in his very next breath says, "but take heart," meaning be encouraged and be comforted because Jesus has overcome the world.

Our human nature is to fear the unknown. God will not lead us to something and then just leave us there. He will supply the courage and confidence we need to overcome. Rely on Him to equip you with what you need at just the right time.

Prayer: Sweet Heavenly Father, you are the epitome of overcoming. Thank you for overcoming death on the cross for me. For me! Father, I need your courage. Take my fears and anxieties away. Give me comfort knowing that you will supply me with whatever I need. I want this small victory. Give me the confidence I need that will help me push through. I'm thankful for your promise that you will show up at just the right time. In Jesus's name, Amen.

Memorize: *Joshua 1:9 NIV: "Have I not commanded you? Be strong and courageous. Do not be afraid; do not be discouraged, for the Lord your God will be with you wherever you go."*

Read: Exodus 3:1–4:31

6
It Takes Time

Walk in wisdom toward outsiders, making the best use of the time.
—Colossians 4:5 (ESV)

I'm sure we can all agree we've said the words, "I don't have time." Surprisingly though, a fun fact I realized is that everybody in the world has twenty-four hours a day to fill how they choose. It's about prioritizing. We make time for what is important to us. We choose how we want or need to fill our days. The key is making good health our priority. I'm reminded of the time I decided to register for a half marathon. Now mind you, I hate running. For some crazy reason, I felt that I could run thirteen miles. The more I trained for it, the more I realized how much time it took me to devote to this event. I'm probably the slowest runner in the world, therefore, it seemed like it took me days to get back home after each run. However, after it was all said and done, setting that time aside so I could best prepare for that race was the best thing I could do.

Exercise Your Faith

Spending time with our Heavenly Father can be just as challenging. You might say, "I'm too busy," "my kids are running around," "it's too noisy," "I'm hardly home," or "I'm too tired." We all have some sort of busyness in our lives. We all have things in our lives that compete for priority. Look at your calendar and you'll see what's important to you. If it's important to us, we will make time for it. My morning routine includes time with Jesus and time for myself. Those are the two most important parts of my day. If I don't have Jesus, I don't have me. And if I don't have me, I can't help or serve anybody else.

Our memory verse for today comes from Matthew (NIV), who encourages us to "seek first His kingdom." We must put Him first in all areas of our lives.

If you don't know where or how to get started, just hold your Bible. Close your eyes. Ask God to show you what to read. Start with a psalm a day. Pick a verse to memorize. All these actions will draw you closer to Him and give you the desire to know Him more.

Prayer: Dear Heavenly Father, show me your awesomeness today. Show me what you want me to see. Speak to me through your Word. Help me understand and hear what you want to say to me today. In Jesus's name, Amen.

Memorize: *Matthew 6:33 NIV: "But seek first his kingdom and his righteousness, and all these things will be given to you as well."*

Read: Ephesians 5:15–16

7
Why Fellowship?

And let us consider how we may spur one another on toward love and good deeds, not giving up meeting together, as some are in the habit of doing, but encouraging one another— and all the more as you see the Day approaching.
—Hebrews 10:24–25 (NIV)

The older I get, I find myself being more introverted than I used to be. I have worked out both by myself and with a group and I'll admit, I prefer to work out by myself. It's easy. It's comfortable and I don't have to socialize. I have my routine. I get up, get dressed, go out and do my thing. However, I know I get a much better workout when I'm with a group. The instructor pushes me just as I push myself more. I also learn different things from other people in the class. It's more encouraging to me because I can tell I'm pushing myself harder and getting a much better workout.

Sometimes it's good to throw some variety in there. Work out with a partner. Join a class. It helps keep you accountable. Knowing that someone is waiting for you and counting on you will surely get you up in the morning. Remember, it may be *you* who is encouraging someone else just by showing up.

Fellowship is like a group class. Proverbs 27:17 NIV reminds us that "as iron sharpens iron, one man sharpens another." We need to be around other believers. It helps us grow and makes us stronger spiritually. We encourage and support each other because of the mutual bond that we Christians share. Just as we have brothers and sisters in real life, we also have brothers and sisters in Christ. Lastly, it reminds us that we're not alone. There's nothing like hearing the congregation singing, worshipping, and praising our God together. Our key verse tells us to "spur one another on towards love and good deeds." What a fun thought!

Try joining a Bible study, small group, or book study. This keeps us accountable as usually there is a schedule to follow with discussion after certain reading assignments. You may also find yourself making more meaningful connections because of the more intimate setting. It is refreshing to find you have more in common with other group members than you ever imagined. You may find the smaller, more focused attention on a topic will give you so much more insight and appreciation than if you were to read something on your own. You'll often hear other ideas, opinions, and perspectives you may not have thought of. I know it's easy to get comfortable and stay home on Sunday morning and say you don't need the church fellowship. I've said that too many times only to come home and say I'm so glad I went.

Robin Urbina

Prayer: Sweet Heavenly Father, you know it's sometimes hard for me to even think about going out, going to church, or just being around other people. Lord, give me the desire to want to go out. Give me the motivation it takes to go out. Use me however you need so that I can encourage someone today. In Jesus's name, Amen.

Memorize: *Philippians 2:2 NIV: "Complete my joy by being of the same mind, having the same love, being in full accord and of one mind."*

Read: Ecclesiastes 4:9–12

8

Endurance

Therefore, since we are surrounded by so great a cloud of witnesses, let us also lay aside every weight, and sin which clings so closely, and let us run with endurance the race that is set before us.
—*Hebrews 12:1 (ESV)*

The definition of endurance is the ability to withstand hardship or adversity. When I think of endurance, I think of the Tarahumara Runners or Ironman Triathlon competitors and the hours of training they go through to prepare. Those hours and hours of training have helped them get to the level they are. They've withstood the hardship and adversity of long hours, physical pain, mental burnout, and time away from family so they can build up their endurance. They do it so they can stand up to whatever obstacles that might get in the way of their training and, ultimately, their races. Building up our tolerance levels is what gets us through the physical pain and mental games we play with ourselves. Registering for a race, triathlon, or even just a ride with a friend keeps me fixed on the event so I know how I need to prepare. It's not just the physical activity; it's knowing how long to train, how to eat properly, how to get enough sleep, how to rest—the whole package.

Being a Christian is the same. It requires us to give up anything that would get in the way of our relationship with God. Today's verse from Hebrews tells us to "lay aside every weight, and sin which clings so closely." We cannot mature and be productive in our spiritual walks when we're carrying the extra weight of sin. It's impossible to focus on God when guilt or shame or other burdens are taking us away from Him.

Just as the athlete fixes his or her eyes on the race, so should we fix our eyes on Jesus; focus on Him, stay the course, and finish victorious.

Prayer: Sweet Heavenly Father, thank You for dying on the cross for me. Thank You for taking the punishment for my sins. You've already endured and run the race. You've already won. Take away the weight of my sins so I can focus on You today. Fill me with Your Holy Spirit so I can endure the race you've given me. In Jesus's name, Amen.

Memorize: *Philippians 4:13 NIV: "I can do all this through him who gives me strength."*

Read: James 1:2–4

9
A Learning Experience

Brothers, I do not consider myself to have taken hold of it. But one thing I do: Forgetting what is behind and reaching forward to what is ahead.
—Philippians 3:13 (HCSB)

I will never forget the time when I was about two minutes from starting my second Olympic distance triathlon that I had spent months preparing for. Anticipation, adrenaline, excitement, and butterflies were all working together making the perfect pre-race cocktail. I knew once I got in the water, I would be fine. It's just something about the five minutes before the start that gets me every time.

We were all standing in the starting line, with all our red swim caps on. I noticed as I was looking around that there were not too many people left in the whole competition. I realized I was in the sprint group and not the Olympic group. Normally the longer distance participants start in the earlier waves. Horrified, I learned my wave had already started twenty-five minutes prior. I was almost nauseous knowing that they close the swim course after a certain time. I knew how long it was going to take me to go the whole distance around the lake. I was not going to make it in time before they closed it. I couldn't make a decision quick enough so I jumped in the water for the sprint start. The whole time I was swimming to the in-water start line, I was trying to hold back my tears. We got to the start line and I had it in my mind I was going to swim past the turn for the sprint course and try to make the full distance swim in time before they closed the course. After swimming about 100 yards past the turn, with disappointment, anger, and frustration, I finally stopped. I couldn't take the stress, heartbreak, and confusion in my head any more. I waved for the official on the jet ski. He came over to me and I explained what happened. He said it was up to me to try or I could have him take me back. Making the decision to get up on that jet ski was harder than all the training I had ever done. Making that ride of shame back to the start line was the worst thing ever, at that moment.

It took a very long time for me to stop beating myself up for missing the correct start time. However, I learned from it and have grown—and haven't missed a start time since.

God has already taken into account my mistakes. I need to quit beating myself up and accept His mercy and grace. I know He has already forgiven me for all of the big, small, stupid, and horrible things I've done. I'm the one who has to forgive myself for them. I'm the one who is punishing myself for carrying all that weight. He's already forgiven me because He loves me unconditionally.

Exercise Your Faith

Today's verse from Philippians 3:13 encourages us to stop looking back and move forward. There is nothing we can do about it now. We can't continue to live there. It's not healthy. We need to realize and accept that God has already forgiven us. Stop holding onto those feelings. It's only distracting you from moving forward and growing your relationship with Him.

Prayer: Father God, I confess and surrender my sins to you. I can't bear them anymore. It pains me to keep reliving them. I don't want to live there any more. Please take the shame and guilt I've been carrying. You know my heart. Take away my distractions. Stop them from interfering during my time with you. I want to move forward with you and not look back. Make today my new beginning. In Jesus's name, Amen.

Memorize: 2 Corinthians 5:17 ESV: "Therefore, if anyone is in Christ, he is a new creation. The old has passed away; behold, the new has come."

Read: Ephesians 4:22-24

10
Love Your Bumps

Therefore, my beloved brothers, be steadfast, immovable, always abounding in the work of the Lord, knowing that in the Lord your labor is not in vain.
—1 Corinthians 15:58 (ESV)

Every time I look in the mirror and see all the dimples and bumps, I honestly don't jump up and down with joy in my heart. It's just not the same as losing a pound or two! I keep wondering if and when they are ever going away. I mean really. I've been exercising for what seems like all my life and I just can't seem to overcome the bumps and dimples. I have noticed, however, that they change. If I'm in a good season, they seem to smooth out and look better. Other seasons, they are maybe a little more bumpy. Finally, I realized if I would just be consistent, keep working out, and make good food choices, the more favorable season would stick around longer. The key is consistency. I have to take care of my body like it is something I love. I have to fall in love with the process of taking care of myself and my body. If I do that, it won't always seem like a battle.

In the process, I'm learning to accept every single flaw and love it the best I can. It is part of me and what makes me me. I love me! Just because I don't see physical results doesn't mean I'm not doing my body good. I know if I just stick with it and continue to make good food choices and continue to move physically, I will see the benefits. Inconsistency opens the door to making excuses and giving up.

Never changing is a great way to describe consistency. God never changes. He doesn't change based on circumstances, like we do. He's reliable. That means we can trust Him. He expects us to be consistent because He is consistent.

If we break down today's verse, the same message applies. To be steadfast means being unwavering, being dedicated, and being committed. Similarly, immovable means to be fixed or stable. "Always abounding" means plentiful, abundant, and overflowing. "The work of the Lord" is all things Jesus: teaching and sharing the Gospel, furthering the kingdom of God, and being an example of Jesus Christ. The last part is the best part: 'Knowing that in the Lord your labor is not in vain." It means that it won't be for nothing. It won't be useless or fruitless.

Now that we know we have to be consistent in the Lord, here are a few ways to stay consistent in your walk.

- Fellowship with other believers
- Make an effort to remove sin from your life
- Reassure your heart by reading your Bible
- Memorize Scripture

- Share your faith with others
- Limit your time with worldly things
- Meet with the Lord daily in prayer

Whatever it looks like for you, know that the Lord sees you. He knows your heart and your intentions. Be diligent, be consistent, and you will be blessed.

Prayer: Dear Lord, thank you for never changing. Thank you for being consistent. I know I can trust you. Help me be more like you. Show me where I can adjust to make more time for you. In Jesus's name, Amen.

Memorize: *1 Timothy 4:15 ESV: "Practice these things, immerse yourself in them, so that all may see your progress."*

Read: Hebrews 10:23

11

Take Time to Heal

He heals the brokenhearted and binds up their wounds.
—Psalm 147:3 (NIV)

When I think of pain, I think of physical and emotional pain. In terms of exercise, physical pain can come from pulled muscles, torn ligaments, and the beloved shin splints. It's not fun working out in pain. (I'm talking about injury pain here, not progress pain.) Oftentimes, it can cause more damage. When I'm in pain, as much as I hate it, I know I have to take time to rest and let my body heal. Sometimes, that can take days or even weeks. However, when I am able to come back, I come back better and stronger.

When I think of emotional pain, I think of heartache, betrayal, grief, shame, failure, and more. I have made too many bad choices in my life. Some hurt so much to this day that I still can't talk about them. If I get too much in my head for too long, I will revisit those mistakes and find myself in a state of depression—again. However, it brings me such peace reading God's Word about healing. I love Psalm 6:2 NIV: "Have mercy on me, Lord, for I am faint; heal me, Lord for my bones are in agony."

It's easy to stay trapped in our trials. So many times, I've cried out to God to take my pain away. When it seems like He's taking forever, I find solace in our key verse from Psalm 147:3 NIV: "He heals the brokenhearted and binds up their wounds." Even just the first part, "He heals the brokenhearted," sounds so comforting. I love saying it: He heals the brokenhearted. He *heals* the brokenhearted. Moreover, he doesn't just heal our broken hearts, he binds up our wounds. He restores us. Nobody knows our hearts and our hurts like Jesus does. We all hurt in our own individual ways but he understands and will comfort us and restore us. All we need to do is let Him.

Prayer: Sweet Heavenly Father, you know me as no one else knows me. You know my physical pain and you know my heartaches. I'm overwhelmed. I ask you to take away this pain. Let me feel your loving arms around me right now. Father, strengthen my thoughts and my mind. Raise me up out of this dark place. Lord, you know it's hard for me to forgive myself and others. I need your help. Help me forgive myself for the pain I've caused. Give me your strength and help me forgive those that have hurt me. In Jesus's name, Amen.

Memorize: Jeremiah 30:17 NIV: "'But I will restore you to health and heal your wounds,' declares the Lord."

Read: Psalm 23

12

Don't be a Quitter

*And let us not grow weary of doing good, for in
due season we will reap, if we do not give up.*
—Galatians 6:9 (ESV)

Have you ever heard the phrase "it's harder to start over than it is to quit"? I cannot count how many times I've started my exercise program from the beginning only to realize I should have never stopped. Many times, I've let too many days go by due to vacations or being sick or because I'm "just not feeling it." Dealing with the challenge of getting up in the morning and the pain that I know I'll endure during the workout *and* after is just as hard as the workout itself. However, I've realized it's easier to keep going. Admittedly, it gets easier to get up early and get it done. I strive to incorporate exercise and my "me time" into my normal everyday life. For me, it has to be a part of my day. Routine. However, if I miss or make a few bad food choices, I feel like I've already failed and think, *Well, I blew it, so who cares? I quit.* No! We can't have that kind of thinking. A few bad meals or a few bad days doesn't ruin your program. Giving up does. Some quit because they don't see progress or it's going too slowly. Nevertheless, even slow progress is still progress.

In today's verse from Galatians 6:9, Paul encourages us to keep doing good and keep going, and we will reap what we sow. I love how he adds "in due season." That means in God's time, He will reward our faithfulness. We will reap what we've sown. Our job is to plant seeds and God's job is to water them and make them grow. Then, in His time, or in "due season," we will reap a harvest of blessings. We will see the fruits of our labor. The Bible teaches us to endure the struggles, to persevere, and to resist the temptations to quit.

Prayer: Heavenly Father, so many times you know I feel like quitting. You know at times I feel completely spent. Your Word says, "I can do all things through Christ who gives me strength" (Philippians 4:13 NIV). Lord, I'm asking for your strength. I can't do this without you. Give me your strength to endure the struggles and temptations I'm facing. I turn this over to you today. Open my heart to accept your help to get me through. In Jesus's name, Amen.

Memorize: *James 1:4 ESV: "And let steadfastness have its full effect, that you may be perfect and complete, lacking in nothing."*

Read: Deuteronomy 31:8

13

Get Energized

Do not be slothful in zeal, be fervent in spirit, serve the Lord.
—Romans 12:11 (ESV)

If I were to ask you if you love yourself, how would you answer? I will honestly say my answer is not always yes. But again, I'm a work in progress. We all are. All too often, we fall into the rut of not having the energy to clean the house let alone exercise. One missed day leads to another and another. Before you know, you're starting all over again. We can't let ourselves slip away. Obviously, we didn't choose our bodies, but we can certainly choose how we treat them. We have to love ourselves and our bodies enough to exercise and care for them.

When I fall into the trap of having no energy, I try to find something that is going to excite me. The thought of getting up just to do crunches and leg lifts doesn't really get me going. However, if you say "let's go hiking or for a long bike ride," I'm all in. Those things work for me. They make me feel alive. I love feeling the wind as I'm pedaling and the quietness of the bike path. I love the challenge of riding my dirt bike over loose rocks and deep sand. I love being in the midst of a workout thinking how awesome it is that my body can actually do certain things. We shouldn't focus on what we can't do. We have to celebrate what our bodies *can* do. It's easy to make time for the things that make us feel alive.

Spiritually, we can fall into the same trap. It's easy to become lukewarm in our walks with the Lord. God doesn't want us to be lazy or idle. As Paul says in Romans 12 (ESV), we are to serve Him with zeal and passion. We are to be diligent in making a continual, honest effort, such as stopping to pray, being thankful before a meal, or praising Him for an answered prayer. Being "fervent in the Spirit" is not about being an outgoing person or involved in every ministry or service opportunity that becomes available. We just need to be passionate about God. People will see that in us and want to know more, which ultimately gives us a chance to share Jesus with someone. When you're excited and passionate about something, it's easy and natural to want to share. Then God will do the rest.

Prayer: Sweet Heavenly Father, thank you for the body you've given me. Today I celebrate what my body can do. Lord, I don't want to be a boring blah lukewarm Christian. I want to celebrate You. Fill me with zeal and passion so I can be enthusiastic and excited to serve you. In Jesus's name, Amen.

Memorize: *Luke 10:27 ESV: "You shall love the Lord your God with all your heart and with all your soul and with all your strength and with all your mind."*

Read: Colossians 3:23-24

14

A Whole Body Workout

Put on the full armor of God, so that you can take your stand against the devil's schemes.
—*Ephesians 6:11 (NIV)*

Recently, a friend invited me to go mountain biking. She assured me it would be a pretty easy trail with only a few inclines and some minor technical spots. I had never been so I thought it might be fun to try. I always love a new challenge. We made our way to the trail and within five minutes, we were riding our bikes in the dirt and sand on a trail not much wider than the tires. I did all I could to stay upright while trying to keep my bike on the trail. The biggest challenge was to not fall into all the cacti surrounding us. As I was trying to maneuver all the sharp hairpin turns, loose rocks, and sand, she was up in front of me whistling "Dixie" and had no idea of the entertainment going on behind her. I haven't even mentioned that I was still trying to breathe throughout the whole thing.

Even with all that, I loved it. I got an amazing full body workout. I got my heart pumping for my cardio workout. My brain was working at full capacity trying to concentrate on the trail and everything surrounding it. My balance and coordination were certainly being tested. Of course, it didn't come without a small element of danger. That's why we ride with helmets, knee and elbow pads, and backpacks with water. We have to be prepared to face whatever comes our way.

Spiritual battles are not all that different from the physical battles we may face. The Armor of God is an analogy in the Bible that describes the protection available to us when the enemy is tempting us with sinful situations. The spiritual "armor" includes six elements.

1. The Belt of Truth (Ephesians 6:14). This means we should hold God's truths close to our body, just like we would wear a belt, and strive to live a life of honesty and integrity.
2. The Breastplate of Righteousness (Ephesians 6:14). To be righteous is to do right in God's eyes. Without righteousness, we leave ourselves vulnerable to the enemy's attacks.
3. The Gospel of Peace (Ephesians 6:15). The Gospel means "good news." Peace means being whole and secure. This passage refers to actions like standing firm and keeping our feet anchored. Standing firm maintains our security in our relationship with God.
4. The Shield of Faith (Ephesians 6:16). The Roman soldiers covered their shields in animal hide and then dipped them in water so when the fiery arrows hit, they would be extinguished. Similarly, our faith

Exercise Your Faith

needs to be continually "dipped" in God's Word for the same protection.
5. The Helmet of Salvation (Ephesians 6:17). Salvation happens the moment we put our faith and trust in Jesus Christ. This element comes from the work of Jesus dying for us but also from own personal journeys with the Lord and our efforts to walk like Jesus walked.
6. The Sword of the Spirit (Ephesians 6:17). The Bible is the literal Sword of the Spirit. It is the strongest weapon we hold. We use it for prayer, for protection, for comfort, and for wisdom. There is nothing more powerful than praying scriptures back to the Lord.

Prayer: Dear Lord, thank you for providing me with full armor! You know the spiritual battles that I'm facing. I pray your truths take over my heart and my words today. Help me to be righteous in your eyes. Let your light shine through me so that others may want to know you. I trust that you are in control of whatever trials come my way. Lord, because of my salvation I know that I can never be separated from you again. Most importantly, help me memorize your Word and keep it safe in my heart. In Jesus's name, Amen.

Memorize: *Ephesians 6:13 NIV: "Put on the full armor of God, so that when the day of evil comes, you may be able to stand your ground, and after you have done everything, to stand."*

Read: Ephesians 6:10–18

15

Give It a Rest

So then, there remains a Sabbath rest for the people of God, for whoever has entered God's rest has also rested from his works as God did from his.
—*Hebrews 4:9–11 (ESV)*

A very important aspect of exercise is rest. Taking a day off or doing a light workout is very beneficial and is just as good as a regular workout. Our bodies need the rest. That is when our muscles recover and refuel. They repair themselves and get stronger. Rest days also help prevent injuries. If we're not on our A-game, it's very easy to be injured. Too much exercise with no rest puts strain on both your body and mind. We can become both physically and mentally exhausted which can snowball into many other issues. I think of athletes training for a marathon who have to be both physically and mentally prepared. If not, serious injuries can occur. I notice this when I'm running. I never realize how beneficial my rest days are until my next run when I go the same distance and actually improve my time. If you are obsessing over exercising or feel tired after a workout, you probably need a day off. Listen to your body.

We get so busy not just with exercise but with everyday life. In Psalm 46:10 NIV, Jesus reminds us to be still and know that He is God. Just as our bodies need to rest, so do our thoughts. We live in a time when everything is right at our fingertips and the pace is nonstop. We need to be still and take time to listen to what God has to say to us. I love looking forward to my quiet time each morning. I enter it knowing it's just me and Him. He is always there waiting for me. I can't wait to see how He's going to speak to me. I'm reminded of a time when I went out of town on a personal retreat. I went to my favorite hiking spot in the woods and rented a cabin for a few days. It was one of the most amazing spiritual experiences of my life, not just the quiet time I had reading my Bible but the overall experience of the downtime, prayer time, and reflection.

The most important thing we can do to "be still" is to just stop. Be intentional. Be alone. Take time to acknowledge our awesome God. Even Jesus "went up on a mountainside by Himself to pray. When evening came, He was there alone" (Matthew 14:23 KJV). Turn off the phone or the TV. Whatever is taking you away from Him, get away from it, even if just for a few minutes. Our quiet time with God doesn't always have to be reading scripture. It can be our prayer time. Take time to thank Him and praise Him for who He is and how He has worked in your life. It can be through music, or writing. Start a journal. Reflect on both the good and bad, remembering that He is working His plan for you.

Robin Urbina

Prayer: Dear Lord, slow me down today. Assure me that it's okay to take a day off. Use this day to draw me closer to you. I need this time to draw nearer to you so I can be refreshed and reenergized to serve you again tomorrow. In Jesus's name, Amen.

Memorize: *Matthew 11:28 NIV: "Come to me, all you who are weary and burdened, and I will give you rest."*

Read: Genesis 2:2–3

16

Stay Hydrated

"But whoever drinks of the water that I will give him will never be thirsty again. The water that I will give him will become in him a spring of water welling up to eternal life."
—John 4:14 (ESV)

So many times, we hear how great water is for us. I've never really struggled with drinking water on a regular basis. I like drinking water. There's nothing like chugging a big glass of water after a good workout. It's refreshing and it quenches my thirst like nothing else. Some say it's boring but it has incredible benefits. For instance:

- It makes your skin soft
- It's cleansing, both inside and out
- It helps you digest food
- It lubricates your joints
- It quenches your thirst

Our bodies lose water throughout the day from moving, sweating, digesting food, and even breathing. That's why we need to hydrate throughout the day and eat foods that help replenish what we've lost. If we don't, we can become dehydrated, which leads to a whole list of serious health conditions.

Spiritually, we need to satisfy that need to know the truth, to be freed from the bondage of guilt and shame, and to be one with God. It's natural for us to seek worldly things to quench that thirst, but God wants us to receive Him so that we can continually be satisfied. Once that happens, "streams of living water" will flow from within us (John 7:38 NIV). This means we will be pointing others to Jesus as a result of our relationship with Him. That is our job as Christians.

We are more than just physical beings. We have souls—thirsty souls. Let's keep them both hydrated and quenched by filling them with the Living Water that the Holy Spirit is offering.

Prayer: Sweet Heavenly Father, thank you for filling me with your Holy Spirit—the Living Water that you gave me to quench my spiritual thirst. Use me to show others the peace and love and kindness that they're longing for. Fill me with your presence so that I can be a light for others. In Jesus's name, Amen.

Memorize: John 7:38 NIV: "Whoever believes in me as the Scripture has said, streams of living water will flow from within him."

Read: John 4:1–26

17

Walking Tall

Since we live by the Spirit, let us keep in step with the Spirit.
—Galatians 5:25 (NIV)

I love finding 5Ks or 10Ks that have a category for walkers. The last 10K I did was in a walker group. Seeing the differences in people, body shapes, and athletic ability always amazes me. If you ever want to be inspired, sign up for some sort of race. When I'm walking, I feel energized. I feel such peace. I get to see God's creation in so many ways. Walking the routes through neighborhoods or on desert trails or an easy walk through the mountains brings such tranquility. Seeing the beauty of wildlife, vegetation, critters, rocks, and running water, I am always amazed by how creative our God is.

God wants to be involved in everything we do, not just spiritually. He cares about our social circles, our physical needs, our thoughts, even our jobs. We need to make sure we are in line with His values.

Robin Urbina

Considering today's topic, what does it mean to keep in step with Jesus? It means to be like him, to have His compassion, and to show His forgiveness to others just as he forgives us.

We can also do this by seeking Him. We seek him by reading His Word and learning about Him. We need to listen. What is He telling you? He'll use His Word to answer. He'll use other people. He'll use objects and experiences. He'll use songs. Other times, keeping in step with Him might look like being led to give financially even if times are tough. It may feel like a little nudge to finally compromise with someone or to forgive someone who has intentionally hurt us. Galatians 5:16 NIV assures us that if we walk by the Spirit, we will not gratify the desires of the flesh. His words will be in us and His love will guide our actions.

Prayer: Dear Heavenly Father, I want to walk in step with you. Help me recognize Your leading so I can walk in Your Spirit. Mold me and fill me with the qualities I need so I can live like you. In Jesus's name, Amen.

Memorize: *Galatians 5:22 NIV:* "*But the fruit of the Spirit is love, joy, peace, forbearance, kindness, goodness, faithfulness,* 23 *gentleness and self-control. Against such things there is no law.*"

Read: 1 Corinthians 13:4-8

18

Just Have Fun

*This is the day that the Lord has made;
let us rejoice and be glad in it.*
—*Psalm 118:24 (NLT)*

I love being in the water, whether it is a pool, a lake, or the ocean. Even if I see a stream, I have to take my shoes off and wade in. I love finding ways to incorporate a good workout in whatever we might be doing. If I'm on a boat, I can't resist jumping in and swimming around. Oftentimes, I'll just swim back to shore.

One day, my son and I were out on the paddleboard. It was a perfect day not just for being on the water but for spending that time with my son. I would sit on one end while he was on the other end doing handsprings then flipping into the water. We created this silly game where we had to try to make the other one fall into the water. We got a great workout in and we didn't even feel like we were exercising. We were just having fun. We could spend hours out there talking, swimming, treading water and, yes, trying to push each other in.

Robin Urbina

Memorizing Bible verses is not like splashing in the water. It's not fun for me. It's hard, especially the long ones! I went to Bible Camp when I was young and, of course, we learned songs to help us memorize verses. I can't help but sing today's verse, Psalm 118:24, every time I see it: "This is the day that the Lord has made. We will rejoice and be glad in it." I have to sing it to the tune by which I learned it. That alone cracks me up! It's such a fun verse and it always makes me smile. Knowing God made this day—today—I will rejoice and be glad in it. I will be thankful for this day.

Joy is an attitude. It's about how we choose to respond to what is put in front of us. I'm not saying we have to smile and be happy and laugh all the time. There's a difference between joyfulness and happiness. I know many things can steal our joy. However, we can't base our joy on circumstances. If we do, we're only setting ourselves up for failure. We can't say "I'll be happy if" or "I'll be happy when." Nehemiah 8:10 NIV reminds us that "the joy of the Lord is our strength." It's much easier to have a joyful heart being guided by faith than to try to muddle through the day with the stresses and cares of the world. He explains in John 15:11 NIV that He wants to give us His joy so that our joy may be complete. What more do we need?

Prayer: Heavenly Father, fill me with your joy today so that mine will be complete. Give me a joyful heart so that I can encourage others. Use me to help somebody smile today. Use my story, my experience to help somebody make it through today. In Jesus's name, Amen.

Exercise Your Faith

Memorize: *Romans 15:13 NIV: "May the God of hope fill you with all joy and peace as you trust in him, so that you may overflow with hope by the power of the Holy Spirit."*

Read: John 15:1–17

19
Persistence Pays Off

Blessed is the one who perseveres under trial because, having stood the test, that person will receive the crown of life that the Lord has promised to those who love Him.
—James 1:12 (NIV)

To be persistent means to do something without ceasing, continually, and with no regard for difficulty or opposition. With this in mind, I think of the first half marathon that I completed quite a few years ago. I look back and grin as I remember wondering how on earth I was going to finish. It was a very hilly course and, of course, very hot. I was about three miles from the finish line. I realized my legs were just going through the motions, putting one foot in front of the other. It was kind of weird but cool. Then I thought about how far I had come and what an awesome personal accomplishment I was experiencing. Even though I thought I had nothing left, I felt like I was doing the rest with just my heart. I couldn't not finish! I had to be persistent and get through those last few miles. I reflected on all the hours of running that I had put in

Exercise Your Faith

to train for this event and I was not going to quit. That consistency, that continual training, was what brought me to that finish line.

Luke 18:2–8 (NLT) contains a parable about a persistent widow. "In a certain town there was a judge who neither feared God nor cared about people." Basically, he was a corrupt judge. A widow continually came to him asking for justice against her adversary. He ignored her pleas for quite some time until he finally got tired of her asking. Finally, because she kept bothering him, the judge granted the justice she was seeking. This illustration does not mean we have to have marathon prayer sessions or keep repeating our prayers and appearing to be a nag to God. It teaches us to be persistent in our prayer life, believing he will answer. The passage ends with Jesus asking, "Will not God bring about justice for his chosen ones, who cry out to him day and night? Will he keep putting them off?" Finally, he assures us and says, "I tell you, he will see that they get justice, and quickly."

Persistence needs to be in every aspect of our faith. That means our service, our relationships, our attitudes, and our reactions to life's challenges. Romans 5:3 (ESV) says, "Not only so, but we also rejoice in our sufferings, because we know that suffering produces perseverance; perseverance, character; and character, hope." Doing so will strengthen our characters and deepen our trust in God.

Prayer: Dear Heavenly Father, I'm trying to stay afloat but I'm tired of this trial. I don't want to do this anymore. I don't understand why you chose me to deal with such challenges. If it's your will, I'll do it. I need your strength to see this through. Give me your wisdom, your understanding, your compassion, and whatever I need to endure this to the end so I can give you the glory. In Jesus's name, Amen.

Memorize: *1 Thessalonians 5:17 ESV: "Pray without ceasing."*

Read: Romans 5:1–8

20

Personal Growth

Practice these things, immerse yourself in them, so that all may see your progress.
—1 Timothy 4:15 (ESV)

For me, there is nothing more satisfying than seeing improvements in my health, whether it be on the inside or on the outside. I take great pleasure in looking at event results, to see my time improve by mere seconds, or to see my blood work results come back with better numbers. That tells me I'm improving, that I did better than the last time. In addition, what else could be more satisfying than feeling better in your clothes? When my jeans feel just a little bit looser, even fresh out of the dryer, it's like a relief that my efforts are paying off. Those little achievements keep me going.

The growth that I see personally in all those examples shows me that I'm growing as a person, as an athlete, as a friend, and as a woman. Every living thing, including me, has its own season for growth, no matter how long or short it may be.

Conversely, I take more pleasure in seeing other people grow. I think of my friend who completed her first relay triathlon. She was still hesitant to enter the event even after I assured her she could do it. To see her come across the finish line with a huge smile on her face was the coolest thing.

When I think about my journey with the Lord, I often feel disappointed in myself because I have failed so many times and wonder if I've really grown. I wonder how can such a loving, forgiving, heavenly Father still love me after all the times I've hurt Him and let Him down. It's because we serve a loving, compassionate and forgiving God.

In 1 Timothy 4, we are instructed to immerse ourselves in 'these things." He's talking about consistent spiritual growth. Imagine a football player. If he doesn't continually train for his sport, he will lose his abilities. He needs to lift weights to become stronger, do some cardio to build his endurance, and probably review plays to keep him mentally sharp so he knows what to do on the field. Just as that athlete loses his abilities if he doesn't continually train, we will not grow spiritually if we do not continually "practice every day."

Spiritual growth can appear to be confidence in knowing that God will work it all out—plain and simple. It can also be having an obedient heart even when our flesh doesn't want to obey. When we learn to rely on the Holy Spirit, our hearts change. Grumbling becomes less, the frustration is set aside, and a little more peace takes over.

Exercise Your Faith

Prayer: Dear Lord, I'm tired of feeling defeated. I'm tired of complaining and all the negativity in my life. Change my heart. Help me see the good in everything today. Show me where I can change so I can serve you better. In Jesus's name, Amen.

Memorize: 2 Peter 3:18 NIV: "But grow in the grace and knowledge of our Lord and Savior Jesus Christ. To him be glory both now and forever! Amen."

Read: Romans 12:6-8

21

Be Creative

Consider it pure joy, my brothers and sisters, whenever you face trials of many kinds, because you know that the testing of your faith produces perseverance.
—James 1:2–3 (NIV)

Those who know me know I can be my own worst critic. I am the first one to beat myself up when I'm not seeing smaller numbers on the scale or my clothes still don't fit. Even though I can't see results yet physically, I know I'm doing my body good. Even if just on the inside for now, I feel good. My confidence is growing. I feel stronger. I'm making better choices throughout the day. I know I'm doing my body and my mind good.

When I'm in a zone like this, I have to keep my momentum going. I can't stop just because I'm not near a gym or I'm out of town or just not feeling it. I should also add that my attention span isn't the longest either. I get bored with doing the same activity for too long, so I've learned I have to be creative. Recently, I had to tend to my dad's

Exercise Your Faith

house while my parents were out of town. They have a pool but it wasn't really long enough to swim laps in. Luckily, my inner ten-year-old appeared quickly. I spent the next thirty minutes running and jumping in the pool and getting out as fast as I could. Needless to say, there wasn't much water left in the pool when I was done, but it was probably one of the best cardio workouts I had done in quite a while.

Sometimes we have to be creative in our worship too. It's easy to get comfortable doing the same things over and over again, but that can get dull. We still need to make sure we "come humbly before Him" (James 4:10 NIV). If you're in church, bow your head or fold your hands together when you pray. Be intentional. Clear your mind of all distractions. Lately, during my quiet time, I've started praying out loud. There's something about hearing myself speak to God that seems to make it more real. Sometimes, I'll even read out loud. I hear what I'm reading and it helps me understand. I also find myself slowing down a bit just to make sure I comprehend what I'm reading. Maybe change the way you approach your prayer time. I'm not saying you *always* have to get on your knees when you pray but at least make an effort to have a humble and quiet heart. (Totally worth it if you have a habit of falling asleep while praying in bed!)

Other little things can make a big difference too. For instance, create opportunities to share Jesus with someone. Display your favorite verse on your desk or make reference to it during conversation. I'm reminded of a few friends who have tattoos of their favorite verses on their arms. Those tattoos have ushered in many questions and conversations about the Lord, some even leading to salvation.

Be creative when witnessing and serving others. He will give you everything you need to plant the seeds He needs to nurture.

Prayer: Dear Lord, I am in awe of you: your grace, your mercy, of who you are. You are the Creator of all creators. Thank you for being such an awesome God! Lord, there are days where I feel like I'm running in place. Father, show me different ways to share Jesus with others. Show me where I can serve you. I am willing to step out of my comfort zone if it means sharing the Gospel. Give me the courage to surrender and be used by you. I trust you to go before me. In Jesus's name, Amen.

Memorize: *Psalm 104:33 KJV: "I will sing unto the Lord as long as I live: I will sing praise to my God while I have my being."*

Read: Romans 12:1–2

22

Just Do It

*Delight yourself in the Lord and He will
give you the desires of your heart.*
—*Psalm 37:4 (ESV)*

The most challenging part of starting a new exercise program is getting up early. If I don't work out in the morning, I don't work out. I'm too tired after work, my feet are swollen, and I'm thinking about dinner. That means I only have one chance to do it. As Arnold Schwarzenegger says, "Just do it. Don't even think about it." With that said, I start mentally preparing the night before. I know I have to tell myself that when I open my eyes in the morning, there is no thinking about whether I'm going to get up or not, I just have to get up. Once I did that for a while, getting up was not difficult any more. Now I can't wait to get up. Sometimes, I wake up before it's time and realize it's way too early to go out and walk or ride or whatever my activity was for the day.

Don't get me wrong—it's not like that every day. Some days it just seems too cold or too dark to get out of bed.

Not everybody is a morning person either. You have to find what fits your schedule and make it work. The second part of this topic about being happy comes *after* the workout. Honestly, I'm not sure if happy describes me as my heart is racing or I'm pushing myself to go harder. Once I'm finished, I feel energized and accomplished knowing I'm one workout closer to my goal. That's when my "happy" sets in.

I understand it's hard to be happy or cheerful if things aren't going our way or how we planned. After all, it's our lives and we should be in control, right? I'd like to say yes, but...no. We can only control so much. The rest is out of our hands. Our happiness depends on how we respond to things. It's a choice. It's easy to let the circumstances or whatever season we are in command the day. That's not healthy. We can't let other people dictate our happiness or feelings. We determine our own happiness.

I do not want to minimize or cheapen life's obstacles and hardships. There are certainly unimaginable things that can test anyone's faith. God does not deny that. He even allows it. It's just comforting to know that while He allows terrible things to happen, He still offers a way to get through whatever trials he brings. Knowing that brings peace and contentment. When we're at peace, we look at things in a different light.

The beginning of Psalm 37:4 says, "Delight yourself in the Lord." That means to enjoy or to take pleasure in the Lord. In today's society, it's easy for us to delight in worldly pleasures, like status or possessions but somehow they always leave us wanting more. We never feel satisfied.

Exercise Your Faith

We can delight ourselves in the Lord by talking to Him more, having a more thankful heart, or even admiring his awesomeness. The second part of that verse says, "He will give you the desires of your heart." The more we align our thoughts with God's, the more it changes our focus and our desires become more like His desires. Those worldly treasures are not as important to us as they used to be.

Look forward to getting to know Him. He *wants* to be known. Talk about Him. Talk to Him. Delight in answered prayer. Delight in His excellence.

Prayer: Father, you are my true source of happiness. I am amazed by your compassion and love for me. Take away my need for worldly approval. Give me an honest heart. Give me a thankful heart. Make the desires of my heart line up with yours. Thank you for loving me the way you do. In Jesus's name, Amen.

Memorize: *Philippians 4:4 KJV: "Rejoice in the Lord always, and again I will say rejoice."*

Read: John 15:10–11

23

But It Hurts

Praise be to the God and Father of our Lord Jesus Christ, the Father of compassion and the God of all comfort, who comforts us in all our troubles, so that we can comfort those in any trouble with the comfort we ourselves receive from God.
—*2 Corinthians 1:3 (NIV)*

It was a Saturday morning. I had ridden my dirt bike Thursday morning for two hours and chose to do a more challenging three-hour ride on Friday. I was spent and already sore. I knew I had to get up and swim because 1) I wasn't going to work out on Sunday, and 2) if I didn't work out, I was going to be more sore the next day. I did all I could to get to the pool. I had nothing mentally or physically. Once I got in, I thought, *Yeah, I guess I can do this.* I continued, and it took everything in me to swim for thirty minutes. I was sore—killer sore. I already knew I wasn't the fastest person in the water (I never am!) but at least I was in it and moving.

I smile when I read Hebrews 12:11–12 (NIV). It says, "No discipline seems pleasant at the time, but painful. Later on, however, it produces a harvest of righteousness and peace for those who have been trained by it." This passage encourages us to lift our drooping hands, strengthen our knees, and make our paths straight so that what is lame will not be put out of joint but rather be healed.

We all have been hurt physically and emotionally. Neither one is fun. I battled depression for years. I was the biggest fake out there and nobody knew what I was going through. I couldn't do anything. I didn't *want* to do anything. I didn't *want* to read my Bible. I didn't even know how to pray anymore, let alone what to pray. Finally, I had to force myself to pick up my Bible. I didn't know what to read or even where to begin again. For a while, all I could do was just open my Bible and cry. God knew my heart. It was just Him holding me as I cried out to him. I got through it, one day at a time, one prayer at a time, one verse at a time.

The pain you feel today is growing into the strength you'll feel and need for tomorrow. It's a building block. God allows trials in our lives so we can grow. We turn them over to Him so that we can use our experiences to help others. He wants us to trust Him. I know that is easy to say and very difficult to do when we are in the depths of pain. I had no love left in me and no love to give to anyone else. How could I praise God? I had nothing to praise Him for. Nevertheless, Paul reminds us in our key verse that our God is the God of compassion and comfort. We may never see the purpose for our suffering but we have to try to hand it over to God. He will equip us and show us how to get through it.

No, it's not fun to do anything while we're hurting. Oftentimes, it feels physically and emotionally impossible. We have to remember there is a season (Ecclesiastes 3:1 NIV) and a reason for everything. Give it to Him and let Him work His plan.

Prayer: Dear Lord, thank you for being the God of comfort and the Father of compassion. Lord, You know my pain. Take my pain, my struggles, my grief, and sorrow from me today, even if just for a day. Let me see Your face and Your work in my life today. I need You today Lord. I need Your strength. Let me feel Your presence today. In Jesus's name, Amen.

Memorize: *Isaiah 41:10 NLT: "Don't be afraid, for I am with you. Don't be discouraged, for I am your God. I will strengthen you and help you. I will hold you up with my victorious right hand."*

Read: Romans 5:1–11

24

Sleep in Peace

When you lie down, you will not be afraid; when you lie down, your sleep will be sweet.
—Proverbs 3:24 (NIV)

Sleep! This is probably my favorite subject! I. Love. Sleep! I even incorporated a statement about sleep into my daily affirmation. That's how important it is.

I actually look forward to going to bed. However my day went, whether good or bad, it has come to an end. It's time to rest my body, my thoughts, and my brain. I try to go to bed around the same time every night. I could probably tell you what time it is just by listening to my body. I also give myself time to wind down so my thoughts aren't keeping me awake when I hit the pillow.

There are many benefits of sleep but we'll just focus on a few. Check these out.

- Sleep helps reduce stress
- It puts you in a better mood

- It helps you think more clearly
- It reduces serious health risks
- It improves productivity
- It improves your memory
- It improves exercise performance

You might say you're too tired to exercise. As weird as it sounds, exercise will improve the quality of your sleep. If you have to exercise when you're tired, just do it. It will work. You will feel more rested when you wake up, allowing you to have a great workout the next day.

Many factors, including worrying, can rob us of a good night's sleep. I understand that and assure you that I've been there too. Worrying is nothing but a way of thinking that leaves you anxious and uneasy and only magnifies the problem. When we worry, we show a lack of faith in God. We show Him we don't trust Him. We need to turn our troubles over to Him to show Him we depend on Him to see things through, whether big or small. If they are important to us, they are important to Him. When He sees that, He will not ignore us.

Worrying is also very harmful to our bodies, both physically and mentally. What we feed our minds determines our levels of stress. We don't need the added pressure of worrying about things we cannot control. Moreover, it hinders our efforts for the moment. We can't be 100 percent when we are consumed by worrying thoughts. Lastly, there may be other challenges God wants us to pursue and worrying keeps us from accomplishing them. Matthew 6:32 NLT reminds us that our "Heavenly Father already knows our needs." Why worry when we can give

Exercise Your Faith

it to Him? We need to be present, in the moment, and rest easy knowing God is in control and will take care of it.

Prayer: Lord, you know my pains. You know my troubles and worries. The worry and stress is exhausting me. Today, I turn them all over to you. I trust your will. I trust whatever plans you have for this situation. Give me sweet rest and let me sleep in peace. In Jesus's name, Amen.

Memorize: *Matthew 7:34 NIV: "Therefore do not worry about tomorrow, for tomorrow will worry about itself. Each day has enough trouble of its own."*

Read: Matthew 6:25–34

25
Reach for It

*Commit to the Lord whatever you do, and
He will establish your plans.*
—*Proverbs 16:3 (NIV)*

I am a list person. I love seeing things checked off showing me how productive I've been. It gives me a sense of accomplishment. I *love* setting goals! It helps me to be intentional in whatever I'm working toward. They give me direction. How can you know what to do or how to proceed if you don't have any direction? In a world full of acronyms, think of FAITH when setting your goals.

The first letter, F, suggests your goals should be *focused*. Think about what you want to accomplish. Is it being able to do a certain activity? Reach a certain weight? Wear a particular suit or dress? Whatever you want to accomplish, write it down. Post it on your mirror, on your fridge, even in your car. Post it anywhere it will remind you of your goal(s) and you'll see it at least once a day.

The A in FAITH stands for *achievable* or *attainable*. You have to set reasonable goals, ones that are realistic. They should also be ambitious and challenging.

The letter I should represent you, the *individual*. Make your goals specific to you. You can't set goals based on someone else's abilities, time frames, or reasons. You know yourself better than anybody else.

T stands for *trackable*. Your goals must be measurable. You need to see what you're doing and how you're doing it. You need to see if you're making progress. This way you'll know how and where to make the necessary adjustments.

H stands for *heartfelt*. You won't accomplish anything unless you truly want it and are willing to work for it. You must be serious and passionate about it. Figure out *why* you're doing this. This is what will drive you to keep going.

Whether our plans are big or small, we are instructed to "commit" whatever we do "to the Lord" (Proverbs 16:3). God wants us to entrust ourselves and our plans to Him. Whatever our plans or goals are, we must trust the Father to do his part in carrying them out, considering it's His will. We all have visions and dreams, but if they do not line up with God's plan, they will not happen. Proverbs 19:21 NIV reminds us, "Many are the plans in a person's heart, but it is the Lord's purpose that prevails." We need to want what the Lord wants.

Now, the fun part: once you have your goals, pray about them. Turn them over to Jesus. Ask Him to help you work through them. Be intentional. Be excited to see how He's going to work. Set small goals. Small goals help you reach bigger goals. Find out what works for you and run with it.

Prayer: Sweet Heavenly Father, thank you for wanting me to succeed. Please help me focus on my goals. I need your strength. I need motivation. Give me the drive that I need to see these goals through. I can't wait to see how you're going to work in my life. In Jesus's name, Amen.

Memorize: *Proverbs 16:9 ESV: "The heart of man plans his way, but the Lord establishes his steps."*

Read: Jeremiah 29:11

26

Invest in Yourself

Do not conform to the pattern of this world but be transformed by the renewing of your mind. Then you will be able to test what God's will is; his good, pleasing and perfect will.
—Romans 12:2 (NIV)

One of the best decisions I ever made was to start working with a food coach. I love the accountability. I need it. It's not always fun, but it keeps me on track.

I've never been one to get my nails done regularly or keep my hair up like I should. However, having a food coach is what works for me. That's my hair and nails splurge. Yes, people say that's not the same thing or that's not any fun. However, that's what I enjoy. I love trying to eat better. I love having someone encourage me or correct me for my own good. I'm investing in myself. I'm choosing what makes me feel good and what keeps me healthy. A side benefit is that a healthy diet produces healthy nails and hair! It's a win-win.

We all like to do things to make ourselves look better and feel better. Some call it self-care. There's nothing wrong with spending time and/or money on ourselves. It's not being selfish. It's okay to take care of yourself. However, we also need to get a little deeper and get that same satisfaction on the inside. Here are some ideas to fill our tanks mentally and spiritually.

- Set healthy boundaries
- See a counselor
- Read a self-help book
- Set a bedtime and stick to it
- Write, then read, your own positive affirmations daily
- Prioritize your time in the Word

God tells us in Mark 12:31 NIV to love our neighbors as ourselves. He wants us to love ourselves. He wants us to care for ourselves as we would care for friends. We can't show God's love to others with depleted energy.

We need to feel good about ourselves and be confident so that we can give our best to God and to others. If it's going to "up your game," be intentional about it and do it. You're worth it.

Prayer: Dear Heavenly Father, you know I sometimes feel guilty about taking time or doing things for myself. Remind me that it's okay to care for myself. I know you want me to care for myself as I would care for others. Sometimes that's hard because there are so many others around me. Help me realize I don't always have to put myself last. I know you want me to be rested and rejuvenated. Help me make space today just for me. In Jesus's name, Amen.

Memorize: *Ephesians 5:29 NIV: "After all, no one ever hated his own body, but he feeds and cares for it, just as Christ does the church."*

Read: Romans 12:4

27
Wait for It

For I know the plans I have for you, declares the Lord, plans for welfare and not for evil, to give you a future and a hope.
—Jeremiah 29:11 (ESV)

How many times do we become frustrated and want to give up on our nutrition or exercise plans just because we haven't seen results yet? For me, the answer is way too many. I try to remember it's not just about reaching a certain number on the scale. It's about being fitter, stronger, and healthier all around. Getting there is a process and it takes time. I know if I keep doing what I'm doing, making progress each day, everything will catch up and come together. My physical health and appearance, my confidence, and overall well-being will improve. Make it about feeling good and strong, fit and confident, and not just about fitting into a smaller dress or pants size.

In Jeremiah 29:11, the Lord tells us that He already knows His plans for us. He wants us to trust in Him and His plan. More importantly, we have to trust in His timing. Just because we may not see visible answers to prayer doesn't mean God isn't working. He may have reasons to make us wait. He may be protecting us from something we're not ready for. We may not be mature enough yet to handle the outcome. Whether we're on the mountain or in the valley, James 1:2–3 (ESV) instructs us to count it all joy when we fall into various trials, knowing that testing our faith produces patience. If it's His plan, He'll let you know. Wait for His answers. Wait for His timing.

Prayer: Dear Heavenly Father, please help me change the way I see myself. Help me realize I'm a work in progress. Father, give me the patience to wait for your answers. Make your will obvious to me so I know how to proceed. In Jesus's name, Amen.

Memorize: *Proverbs 19:21 NIV: "Many are the plans in a person's heart, but it is the Lord's purpose that prevails."*

Read: Romans 8:28–39

28

A Balancing Act

But you, O Lord, are a God merciful and gracious, slow to anger and abounding in steadfast love and faithfulness.
—Psalm 86:15 (ESV)

I've recently come out of a season where I had to do something I've never done before. It was difficult to manage mentally and emotionally and, at a few points, even physically. A lot of the time, I was disgusted and embarrassed to be put in the situation I was in. Other times, I felt sorry. But most of the time, I was stressed out, frustrated, angry, and even hateful. I felt angry and selfish because it turned into a big distraction that took me away from myself, my workouts, and my quiet time with the Lord. I didn't like the fact that it gave me a not-so-loving or unChrist-like attitude. Sadly, all this was only over a four-month period of time.

Sometimes, we are put in positions where we have to deal with a difficult personality or situation. It's hard to be gracious, let alone *speak* graciously when we watch people treat others badly. I will be the first to admit that I was not born with the gift of compassion. I'm still learning to manage my facial expressions better because they speak louder than my words. It's not always easy to hide thoughts or reactions, especially in a challenging situation or conversation.

At some point, we have to take action. In order to keep our own sanity, we have to make sure we are being nice to ourselves so that we can be nice to others. More importantly, we need to stand up for what we believe in. We shouldn't have to compromise our values just to help or please others. We've all heard the saying "put on your own oxygen mask first." This may look like removing ourselves from a situation. Our health and our sanity should be our number one priorities. If it means ridding our lives of toxic people or situations, then so be it. It also could mean saying "no" more often and choosing which situations we want to be in or which situations we should avoid.

Our key verse from Psalm 86 is a great reminder for us to be "slow to anger." It takes a lot for me to become angry, which seldom happens. When I do become angry, I am actually angrier over the fact that I'm angry. I don't like the negative energy that takes over my being. The second part of the verse, "abounding in steadfast love and faithfulness," says we need to be full or abundant in unwavering love. We need to choose words (and the tone in which they're delivered) that will usher in peace, understanding, and patience.

It's quite the balancing act. We need to do what works for us while still being nice to ourselves and others. We also need to be sure to not lose ourselves in the journey.

Robin Urbina

Prayer: Dear Heavenly Father, please forgive me for my bitter attitude. Help me speak graciously when my flesh doesn't want to. Give me a sincere heart and kind words to help me through this situation. Replace my anger and frustration with a loving heart and your sweet compassion. In Jesus's name, Amen.

Memorize: *James 1:19 ESV: "Know this, my beloved brothers: let every person be quick to hear, slow to speak, slow to anger."*

Read: Colossians 3:1–17

29
It Takes Discipline

*For the Spirit God gave us does not make us timid,
but gives us power, love and self-discipline.
—2 Timothy 1:7 (NIV)*

Throughout your lifetime, you see many stories of people who have reached incredible milestones. Some are physical, educational, or even financial. The one thing these have in common is that they all take discipline. Someone pursuing a college degree has to be disciplined enough to show up for class and do the work. If you're trying to pay off your home or save for something special, you make a plan and stick to it, oftentimes sacrificing in other areas so you can reach your goal.

As with any exercise or nutrition plan, you have to have the same discipline. Sure, it's hard to stick to a schedule of exercise or follow a certain meal plan, but that's what discipline is: training yourself to obey the rules you've set for yourself. I love that. It's an easy concept but difficult to execute. We set the rules based on what we want and then work through them one day at a time. For me, it's more like one meal at a time or even one hour at a time.

The first types of discipline I mentioned were preventive and supportive. A third form of discipline is corrective. One example that comes to mind would be a parent correcting a child's behavior. We do this because we love them, we want to keep them safe, and we want to mold good behavior and character. (I chuckle when I look back at my childhood and try to recount the number of times I was grounded.) Our Heavenly Father does the same thing with us out of love. He wants to correct and shape His children into people with His character.

There will always be consequences to our actions, especially if we do something or have hearts not in line with God's values. However, God wants to be the first one to forgive us. He even tells us He will not hold our sins against us (Isaiah 43:25 NLT). All we have to do is ask for His forgiveness. Yes, even if we ask for forgiveness for the same thing repeatedly, we *must* have repentant hearts and do our best to change our behaviors.

Fitness, good nutrition, and a faithful walk with Jesus take discipline. It's not a destination—it's a way of life. Decide what you want and how you want to live and make your rules. Learn to be disciplined and intentional in all areas of your life.

Prayer: Dear Lord, thank you for being my Heavenly Father. I welcome your conviction and correction. Show me where I have unpleasing thoughts in your eyes and help me correct them. Give me the self-discipline that I need to help me reach my goals spiritually and physically. Take away my fleshly desires so that I can get through this day with a victory. Give me your strength to get through each day by being intentional with the goals I've set before me. In Jesus's name, Amen.

Memorize: *Proverbs 22:6 ESV: "Train up a child in the way he should go: and when he is old, he will not depart from it."*

Read: Hebrews 12:4–13

30
It's a Narrow Road

"Enter by the narrow gate; for wide is the gate and broad is the way that leads to destruction, and there are many who go in by it. Because narrow is the gate and difficult is the way which leads to life, and there are few who find it."
—Matthew 7:13–14 (NKJV)

Anyone who has shared a swim lane with me knows I cannot swim the backstroke in a straight line. It's hilarious. I go from one side to the other like a pinball, up and down the lane and back again. To make matters worse, it's another game trying to avoid the painful surprise of hitting the lane rope.

We've all heard the term "walk the straight and narrow." Jesus instructs us in Matthew 7:13 to "enter through the narrow gate." The "narrow" gate referred to here is Jesus. If we purposely live a life pleasing to Jesus, we will find peace and joy that can fill any voids in our hearts. The "broad" way is a life without Jesus, which can be filled with bitterness, unforgiveness, and disappointment.

Exercise Your Faith

It's easy to want to choose the broader way because of our sin natures. The world almost welcomes it. It feels good. It's easy. We all like to be socially accepted. We are diverted because we give in to temptation. We're impatient and we want to do what we want, when we want. That's why we need Jesus (the lane ropes) to keep us where we need to be: in walks that honor and respect God and His values. The more we "stay in our lanes," and walk the way of Jesus, the more our hearts change and the desire to honor God grows stronger.

Prayer: Dear Lord, your Word says the pathway to Heaven is narrow and the pathway to Hell is wide. I choose the narrow. Direct me to that path and help me stay on it. I'm tired of wandering aimlessly. I need you to show me your way. Keep me focused on you and not on what feels good or what's easy and accepted. In Jesus's name, Amen.

Memorize: *Proverbs 28:18 ESV: "Whoever walks in integrity will be delivered, but he who is crooked in his ways will suddenly fall."*

Read: Colossians 1:10

In Closing

Fitness and good health are not destinations. They are ways of life. I have tried many different eating plans or exercise crazes, but I'm still learning it's all just a way of life. It's that simple. As long as I stay consistent and follow a plan, I will still be headed in the right direction. It's simply a lifestyle.

So is our faith, our walks with the Lord. Every day is not always easy, but having His Holy Spirit guiding us helps. It's a continual process of growing with integrity and character as human beings and as children of God. That is something the scale cannot measure.

We live in an evil and corrupt world in a divided society. The world wants us to evolve with it and stray from walking in God's truth, but Philippians 3:20 NIV reminds us that "our citizenship is in heaven." Until we are called to Heaven, we are to set our minds on things that are above (Colossians 3:1 NIV) and to keep our hearts focused on Jesus. To God, our faith is more precious and valuable than gold (1 Peter 1:7 ESV). He wants us. He wants to forgive us and he wants to bless us, because that's the kind of loving, merciful God he is.

You are here to fulfill a purpose. If you are alive, you can be used. All you have to do is be willing. Seek Him and you will find Him.

You will seek me and find me when you seek me with all your heart.
—Jeremiah 29:13 (NIV)

Final Thoughts and Encouragement

I hope you have acquired at least a small nugget of encouragement from these pages. My prayer for you is that you continue in your journey growing closer to God all while challenging yourself physically, mentally, and spiritually. I pray you surround yourself with those who build you up, lift you up, and even ones who hold you up. You are a masterpiece created by God. You are loved more than you know.

If you feel the Lord speaking to you, offering His hand to you, and you are ready to invite Him into your life and trust Him in all things, please read this prayer with your heart so you can receive the greatest gift of salvation:

Dear Lord, I confess that I have sinned. I know that my sin has separated me from you. But I know that I can be forgiven by the death of Jesus on the cross. I believe you died on the cross and rose again to pay the price for my sins. Today I put my faith and trust in you. I invite you into my life and I turn from my sin, so that I can live for you. In Jesus's name, Amen.

If you sincerely prayed that prayer, please tell someone. Tell your family. Tell your friends. Tell me! Seek out a Bible-believing church. This will help you to know where and how to start your Christian walk. Welcome to the family of God.

But to all who did receive him, who believed in his name, he gave the right to become children of God.
—John 1:12 (ESV)

Key Verses

1. "Then He said to the man, 'Stretch out your hand!' He stretched it out, and it was restored to normal, like the other" (Matthew 12:13 ESV).

2. "But he answered, 'It is written, "Man shall not live by bread alone, but by every word that comes from the mouth of God"'" (Matthew 4:4 NIV).

3. "Worship the Lord with gladness; come before him with joyful songs" (Psalm 100:2 NIV).

4. "Do you not know that your body is a temple of the Holy Spirit within you, whom you have from God? You are not your own, for you were bought with a price. So glorify God in your body" (1 Corinthians 19–20 ESV).

5. "I have said these things to you, that in me you may have peace. In the world you will have tribulation. But take heart; I have overcome the world" (John 16:33 NIV).

6. "Walk in wisdom toward outsiders, making the best use of the time" (Colossians 4:5 ESV).

7. "And let us consider how we may spur one another on toward love and good deeds, **25** not giving up meeting together, as some are in the habit of doing, but encouraging one another— and all the more as you see the Day approaching" (Hebrews 10:24–25 NIV).

8. "Therefore, since we are surrounded by so great a cloud of witnesses, let us also lay aside every weight, and sin which

clings so closely, and let us run with endurance the race that is set before us" (Hebrews 12:1 ESV).

9. "Brothers, I do not consider myself to have taken hold of it. But one thing I do: Forgetting what is behind and reaching forward to what is ahead" (Philippians 3:13 HCSB).

10. "Therefore, my beloved brothers, be steadfast, immovable, always abounding in the work of the Lord, knowing that in the Lord your labor is not in vain" (1 Corinthians 15:58 ESV).

11. "He heals the brokenhearted and binds up their wounds" (Psalm 147:3 NIV).

12. "And let us not grow weary of doing good, for in due season we will reap, if we do not give up" (Galatians 6:9 ESV).

13. "Do not be slothful in zeal, be fervent in spirit, serve the Lord" (Romans 12:11 ESV).

14. "Put on the full armor of God, so that you can take your stand against the devil's schemes" (Ephesians 6:11 NIV).

15. "So then, there remains a Sabbath rest for the people of God, for whoever has entered God's rest has also rested from his works as God did from his" (Hebrews 4:9–11 ESV).

16. "But whoever drinks of the water that I will give him will never be thirsty again. The water that I will give him will become in him a spring of water welling up to eternal life" (John 4:14 ESV).

17. "Since we live by the Spirit, let us keep in step with the Spirit" (Galatians 5:25 NIV).

18. "This is the day that the Lord has made; let us rejoice and be glad in it" (Psalm 118:24 NLT).

19. "Blessed is the one who perseveres under trial because, having stood the test, that person will receive the crown of life that the Lord has promised to those who love Him" (James 1:12 NIV).

20. "Practice these things, immerse yourself in them, so that all may see your progress" (1 Timothy 4:15 ESV).

21. "Consider it pure joy, my brothers and sisters, whenever you face trials of many kinds, because you know that the testing of your faith produces perseverance" (James 1:2–3 NIV).

22. "Delight yourself in the Lord and He will give you the desires of your heart" (Psalm 37:4 ESV).

23. "Praise be to the God and Father of our Lord Jesus Christ, the Father of compassion and the God of all comfort, who comforts us in all our troubles, so that we can comfort those in any trouble with the comfort we ourselves receive from God" (2 Corinthians 1:3 NIV).

24. "When you lie down, you will not be afraid; when you lie down, your sleep will be sweet" (Proverbs 3:24 NIV).

25. "Commit to the Lord whatever you do, and your plans will succeed" (Proverbs 16:3 NIV).

26. "Do not conform to the pattern of this world but be transformed by the renewing of your mind. Then you will be able to test what God's will is; his good, pleasing and perfect will" (Romans 12:2 NIV).

27. "For I know the plans I have for you, declares the Lord, plans for welfare and not for evil, to give you a future and a hope" (Jeremiah 29:11 ESV).

28. "But you, O Lord, are a God merciful and gracious, slow to anger and abounding in steadfast love and faithfulness" (Psalm 86:15 ESV).

29. "For the Spirit God gave us does not make us timid, but gives us power, love and self-discipline" (2 Timothy 1:7 NIV).

30. "Enter by the narrow gate; for wide is the gate and broad is the way that leads to destruction, and there are many who go in by it. Because narrow is the gate and difficult is the way which leads to life, and there are few who find it" (Matthew 7:13–14 NKJV).

Memory Verses

1. "But those who hope in the Lord will renew their strength. They will soar on wings like eagles; they will run and not grow weary, they will walk and not be faint" (Isaiah 40:31 NIV).

2. "No temptation has overtaken you except what is common to mankind. And God is faithful; he will not let you be tempted beyond what you can bear. But when you are tempted, he will also provide a way out so that you can endure it" (1 Corinthians 10:13 NIV).

3. "Jesus said to him, 'Away from me, Satan! For it is written: "Worship the Lord your God, and serve him only"'" (Matthew 4:10 NIV).

4. "Jesus answered and said to him, 'If anyone loves Me, he will keep My word; and My Father will love him, and We will come to him and make Our abode with him'" (John 14:23 NASB).

5. "Have I not commanded you? Be strong and courageous. Do not be afraid; do not be discouraged, for the Lord your God will be with you wherever you go" (Joshua 1:9 NIV).

6. "But seek first his kingdom and his righteousness, and all these things will be given to you as well" (Matthew 6:33 NIV).

7. "Complete my joy by being of the same mind, having the same love, being in full accord and of one mind" (Philippians 2:2 NIV).

8. "I can do all this through him who gives me strength" (Philippians 4:13 NIV).

9. "Therefore, if anyone is in Christ, he is a new creation. The old has passed away; behold, the new has come" (2 Corinthians 5:17 ESV).
10. "Practice these things, immerse yourself in them, so that all may see your progress" (1 Timothy 4:15 ESV).
11. "But I will restore you to health and heal your wounds,' declares the Lord" (Jeremiah 30:17 NIV).
12. "And let steadfastness have its full effect, that you may be perfect and complete, lacking in nothing" (James 1:4 ESV).
13. "You shall love the Lord your God with all your heart and with all your soul and with all your strength and with all your mind" (Luke 10:27 ESV).
14. "Put on the full armor of God, so that when the day of evil comes, you may be able to stand your ground, and after you have done everything, to stand" (Ephesians 6:13 NIV).
15. "Come to me, all you who are weary and burdened, and I will give you rest" (Matthew 11:28 NIV).
16. "Whoever believes in me as the Scripture has said, streams of living water will flow from within him" (John 7:38 NIV).
17. "But the fruit of the Spirit is love, joy, peace, forbearance, kindness, goodness, faithfulness, 23 gentleness and self-control. Against such things there is no law" (Galatians 5:22 NIV).
18. "May the God of hope fill you with all joy and peace as you trust in him, so that you may overflow with hope by the power of the Holy Spirit" (Romans 15:13 NIV).
19. "Pray without ceasing" (1 Thessalonians 5:17 ESV).

20. "But grow in the grace and knowledge of our Lord and Savior Jesus Christ. To him be glory both now and forever! Amen" (2 Peter 3:18 NIV).

21. "I will sing unto the Lord as long as I live: I will sing praise to my God while I have my being" (Psalm 104:33 KJV).

22. "Rejoice in the Lord always, and again I will say rejoice" (Philippians 4:4 KJV).

23. "Don't be afraid, for I am with you. Don't be discouraged, for I am your God. I will strengthen you and help you. I will hold you up with my victorious right hand" (Isaiah 41:10 NLT).

24. "Therefore do not worry about tomorrow, for tomorrow will worry about itself. Each day has enough trouble of its own" (Matthew 7:34 NIV).

25. "The heart of man plans his way, but the Lord establishes his steps" (Proverbs 16:9 ESV).

26. "After all, no one ever hated his own body, but he feeds and cares for it, just as Christ does the church" (Ephesians 5:29 NIV).

27. "Many are the plans in a person's heart, but it is the Lord's purpose that prevails" (Proverbs 19:21 NIV).

28. "Know this, my beloved brothers: let every person be quick to hear, slow to speak, slow to anger" (James 1:19 ESV).

29. "Train up a child in the way he should go: and when he is old, he will not depart from it" (Proverbs 22:6 ESV).

30. "Whoever walks in integrity will be delivered, but he who is crooked in his ways will suddenly fall" (Proverbs 28:18 ESV).

Notes

Notes

Printed in the USA
CPSIA information can be obtained
at www.ICGtesting.com
LVHW040940191024
794271LV00030B/293